The Complete List Of Magical Plants & Herbs

And Their Incredible Properties

Crafty Witch

Plant magic is an age old art form that reaches it's occult roots all the way back to ancient Egyptian times... used for many purposes such as healing, self empowerment, love and lust spells and protection... each plant has its own magical properties and strengths and can be used to add power to any kind of spell... plant magic will have the desired result regardless of the power of the person casting the spell due to the fact the plants themselves have high levels of magical properties contained within their very fibres.

With its multiple uses and the speed and effectiveness of its power, plant magic is one of the most popular mystic arts used today.

It's simple... when casting any spell you just choose the plant which holds the same (or similar) properties to that of the spell you are attempting, and your magic will be infinately enhanced.

This short book contains a complete list of these incredible plants and herbs... It has been kept basic and simple so that even the most novice of novices can take advantage of it's contents.

Acacia (Acacia Nilotica) a.k.a. gum arabic.

Gender: Masculine, Planet: Sun, Element: Air, Deities: Osiris, Astarte, Diana, Ra.

Protection, Psychic Powers.

Burn with sandalwood to open psychic centers.

Parts used: dried gum, leaves, wood

Aconite (Aconitum Napellus) a.k.a. wolfsbane, monkshood, blue rocket

POISON Don't ingest.

Gender: Feminine, Planet: Saturn, Sign: Capricorn, Element: Water, Deities: Hecate, Medea.

Protection, Invisibility.

Use this herb with great caution to consecrate the athame or ritual knife. Make an infusion with the leaves or root to banish prior energy from magickal blades and to infuse it with protection. The root or leaves may be burned as incense for the same purpose. Gather the fresh flowers to make a tincture to refresh the power of the knives. Use an infusion as a magickal wash for ritual tools or sacred space. Brings protection and magickal watchfulness against negative energies in ritual. Wash a new cauldron in the infusion or burn aconite in its first fire. Used to invoke Hecate. Wrap the seed in a lizard skin and carry to become invisible at will. Used to poison arrow tips in early times. Also as protection from and a cure for werewolves.

African Violet (Saintpaulia ionantha)

Gender: Feminine, Planet: Venus, Element: Water

Spirituality, Protection.

Promotes spirituality when grown in the home.

Agaric(Amanita muscaria) aka magic mushroom, redcap, death angel, death cap

Gender: Masculine, Planet: Mercury, Element: Air, Deity: Dionysus

Fertility.

Place on the altar or in the bedroom to increase fertility.

Agrimony(Agrimonia eupatoria) Also called Church steeples, cocklebur, stickwort, sticklewort

Gender: Masculine, Planet: Jupiter, Element: Air

Protection, Sleep.

Agrimony is best known for its sleep-inducing qualities, therefore it is excellent in dream pillows, especially mixed with mugwort. Enhances magickal healing. A wash or oil increases effectiveness of all forms of ritual healing, psychic healing, or distance healing. Anoint hands with oil to cleanse auras. Creates a barrier against negative energies. Use if you feel to be under psychic attack. A counter-magick herb, it not only breaks hexes, but sends them back to the hexer.

Alfalfa(Medicavo Sativa)

Gender: Feminine, Planet: Venus, Element: Earth

Prosperity, Anti-hunger, Money.

Brings in money and protects against financial misfortune. Harvest a small quantity at the full moon. Dry and burn in the cauldron. Place ashes in an magickal amulet.

Allspice(Pimenta officinalis or P. dioica)

Masculine, Mars, Fire

Money, Luck, Healing.

Almond(Prunus dulcis)

Masculine. Mercury. Air. Deities: Attis, Mercury, Thoth, Hermes

Money, Prosperity, Wisdom.

Use oil, wash, or incense to anoint magickal wands or ritual candlesticks. (Almond wood makes excellent wands, especially for use in love magick). Excellent herbs for handfastings or other rituals of union. Also good for overcoming alcohol dependency. Almonds, leaves, and wood may be used in money magick. Placing almonds in your pocket will lead you to treasures.

Aloe(Aloe vera) aka burn plant, medicine plant

Feminine. Moon. Water.

Protection, Luck.

Guards against evil influences and prevents household accidents. Plant aloe on the graves of loved ones to promote a peaceful existence until the deceased is reborn. Use for success in the world. Prevents feelings of loneliness.

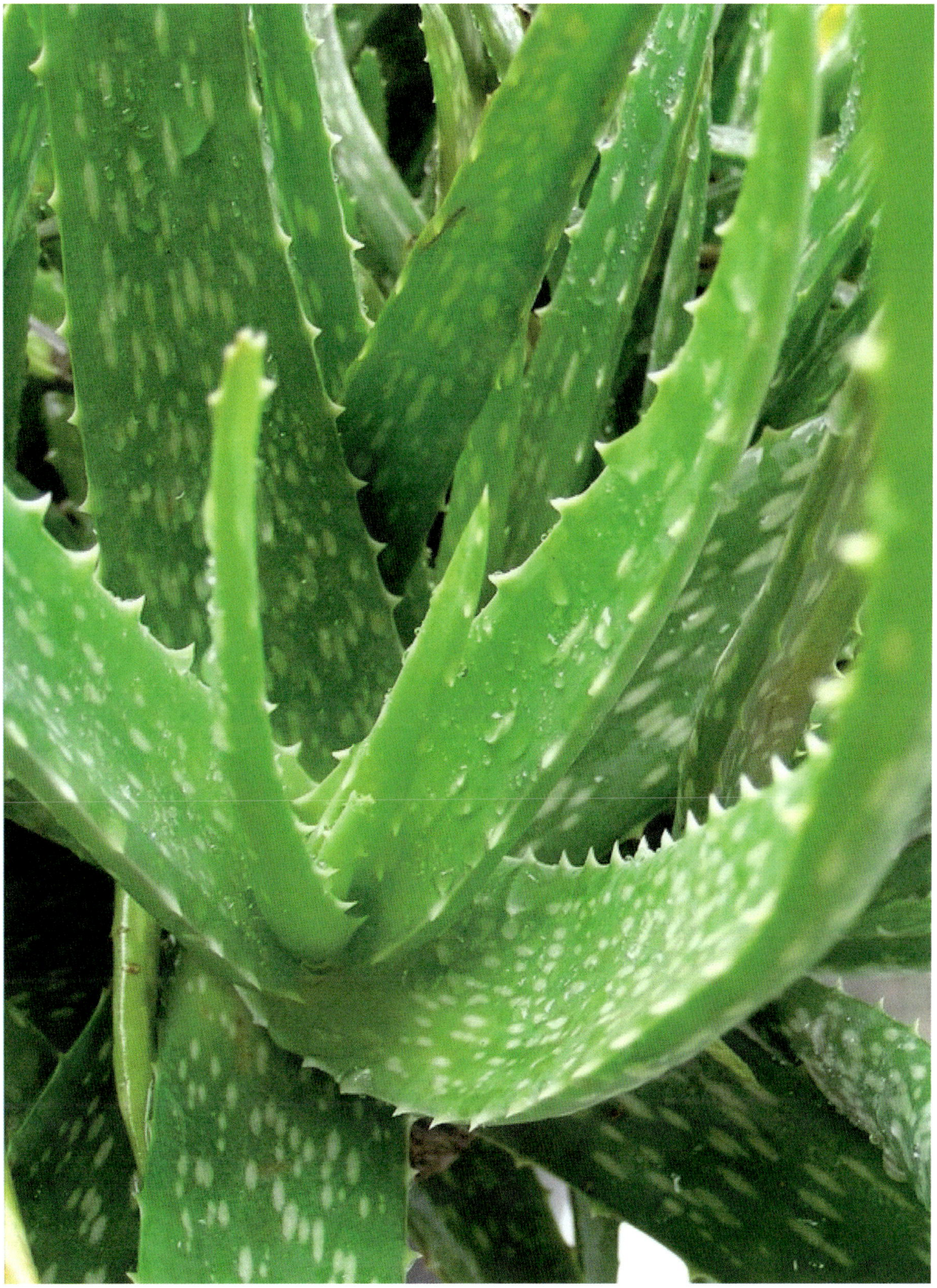

Aloes, Wood(Aquilaria agallocha) a.k.a. Lignum aloes

Feminine. Venus. Water.

Love, Spirituality.

Althea(Althea officinalis) a.k.a. marshmallow, sweet weed, wymote

Feminine. Venus. Water.

Protection, Psychic Powers.

Burn as incense or carry as a sachet for a good psychic power stimulator. A good "spirit puller." It draws good spirits into workings and rituals when placed on the altar. An aphrodisiac — make an oil from seeds gathered under the full moon to use on the genitals. An amulet made of the leaf or root worn near the genitals will accomplish the same ends.

Alyssum(Alyssum spp.) a.k.a. Alison, Madwort

Protection, Moderating Anger

Amaranth(Amaranthus hydrochondriacus) Love-lies-bleeding, red cockscomb, velvet flower

Feminine. Saturn. Fire. Deity: Artemis

Healing, Protection, Invisibility.

Used in pagan burial ritutals. Mends a broken heart.

Anemone(Anemone pulsatilla) a.k.a. Meadow Anemone, Wind Flower, Pasque Flower

Masculine. Mars. Fire. Deities: Adonis, Venus.

Health, Protection, Healing.

Use the blossoms in all healing rituals. Grow red anemones in the garden to protect the garden and the home. Wrap flowers in a red cloth and wear or carry to prevent disease. Use the flowers to color Ostara eggs.

Anemone(Wood) (Anemone nemorosa) a.k.a. crowfoot, windflower

Mars. Deities: Adonis, Anemos, Aphrodite, Eurus, Venus

Healing.

Used to invoke elemental air. Maturing flower is ideal nesting place for faeries. A charm against fevers. Use during rituals of death and dying.

Angelica(Angelica archangelica) a.k.a. archangel, masterwort

Masculine. Sun. Fire. Deity: Venus.

Exorcism, Protection, Healing, Visions.

Use in all protection and exorcism incenses. Angelica protects in two ways: it creates a barrier against negative energy and fills you with good, radiant energy. Removes curses, hexes, or spells that have been cast against you. Enhances the aura. Gives a joyful outlook on life.

Anise Seed(Pimpinella anisum) a.k.a. aniseed, anneys

Masculine. Jupiter. Air. Deities: Apollo, Mercury.

Protection. Purification. Youth.

Deals with inner, personal issues related to lack of fulfillment. Helps one to become more open to happiness and enjoy company of others. Put in dream pillows to protect from nightmares. Brings protection when traveling in the astral. Include anise in handfasting and wedding cakes.

Anise, Star(Illicium verum) a.k.a. Chinese anise

Moon, Uranus. Aquarius.

Use to consecrate ritual cups and chalices. Powdered stars may be used as incense to invoke your Deities or banish negative energy. Used in death and dying rituals.

Apple(Pyrus spp.) a.k.a. Silver bough, silver branch, tree of love

Feminine. Venus. Water. Deities: Pomona, Venus, Dionysus, Olwen, Apollo, Hera, Athena, Aphrodite, Diana, Zeus, Iduna

Love, Healing, Garden Magick, Immortality.

Use apple branches to make wands ideally suited for emotional and love magick. The apple branch will gain one admittance to the faery underworld. For healing, cut an apple into three pieces, rub on the afflicted part of the body, and bury outside. Do this during the waning moon to banish illness. Apples can be used for poppets or the apple wood carved into a poppet. Powder dried seeds and bark to burn as incense. (Caution: more than a few apple seeds can be poisonous). Apples are associated with the dead and Samhain, which is often called the Feast of Apples.

Apricot (Prunus armeniaca)

Feminine. Venus. Water. Deities: Venus

Love.

Use juice in love spells or potions. Eat fruit to obtain a sweet disposition. Leaves and flowers can be added to love sachets and the pits carried to attract love.

Arabic Gum(Acacia vera) a.k.a. Arabic, Egyptian gum, Indian gum

Masculine. Sun. Air.

Purifies negativity and evil.

Add to incense for good vibrations. See Acacia.

Arbutus(Arbutus unede)

Masculine. Mars. Fire. Deity: Cardea.

Exorcism, Protection.

Protects little children.

Arrow Root (Maranta arundinaceae)

Jupiter.

Increases one's good fortune and makes opportunity more visible on the horizon.

Asafoetida(Ferula Foetida) a.k.a. Devil's dung, food of the gods

Masculine. Mars. Fire.

Exorcism, Purification, Protection.

Horrid odor. Use with caution. Used by those seeking the mysteries of the Horned God. Helps us break free of our negative desires. Increases the power of any ritual.

Ash(Fraxinus excelsior or F. americana) a.k.a. Nion

Masculine. Sun. Fire. Deities: Uranus, Poseidon, Thor, Woden, Neptune, Mars, Gwydion

Protection, Prosperity, Sea Rituals, Health.

The Teutonic World Tree, Yggdrasil, is said to be an ash tree. An ash staff wards off evil. Healing wands should be made of ash wood. Carve poppets from the roots of the ash tree. Burning ash at Yule brings prosperity. Carry the leaves to gain love.

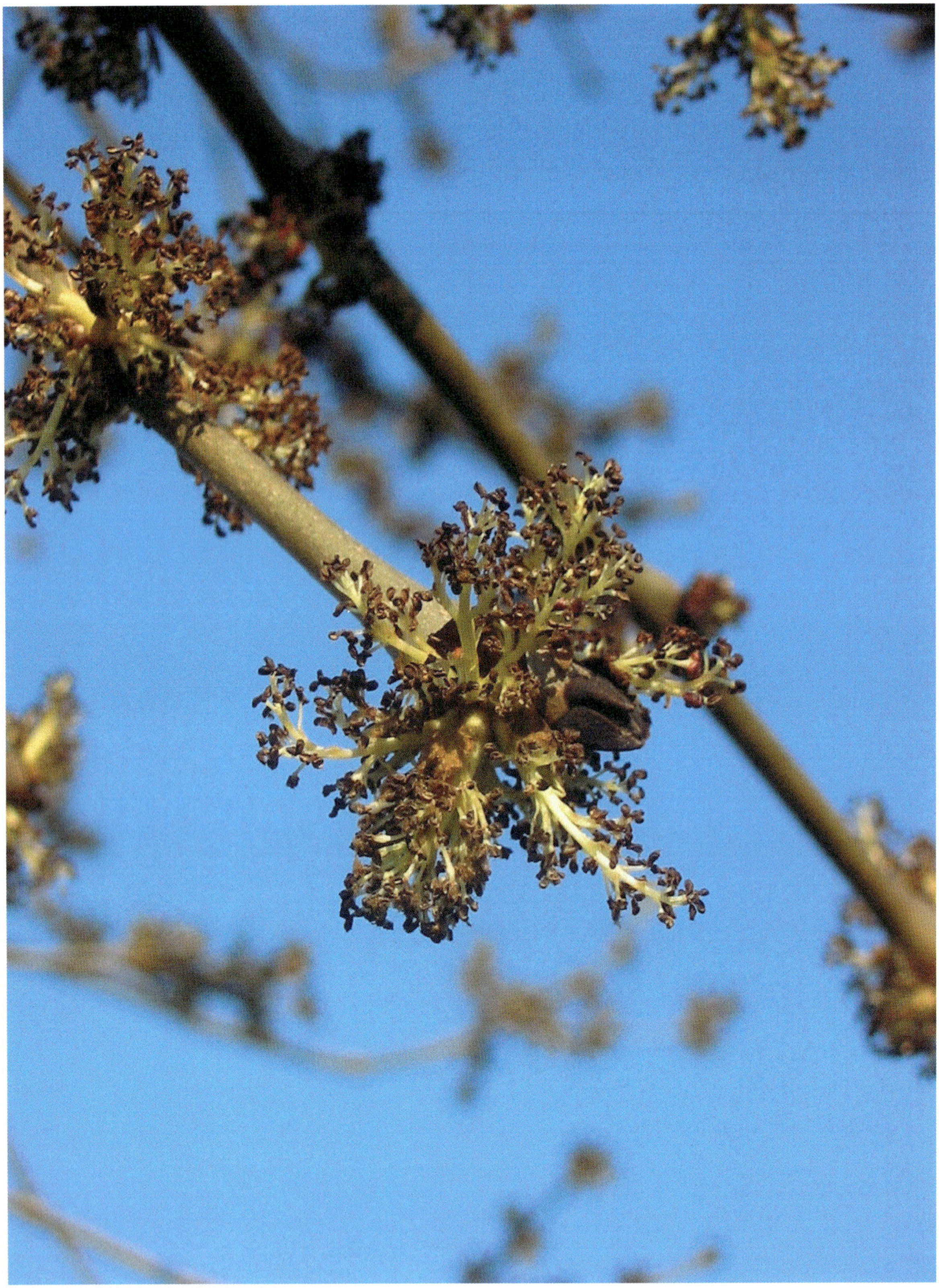

Aspen(Populus spp.)

Masculine. Mercury. Air.

Eloquence, Anti-Theft.

Aster(Callistephus chinesis) a.k.a. China Aster, Michaelmas Daisy, Starwort

Feminine. Venus. Water. Deity: Venus.

Use in love sachets, or carry the bloom to win love. Grow in the garden with a wish for love.

Avens(Geum urbanum) a.k.a. bennet, blessed herb, clove root, golden star, harefoot

Masculine. Jupiter. Fire.

Exorcism, Purification, Love.

Brings protection to the home, kindred, and self. A whole root is needed for an amulet. Burn ground or cut root to promote blessings and keep out negativity.

Avocado(Persea americana) a.k.a. alligator pear

Feminine. Venus. Water.

Love, Beauty, Lust.

Grow a plant from the pit of an avocado to bring love into it. Wands made from avocado wood make potent all-purpose instruments.

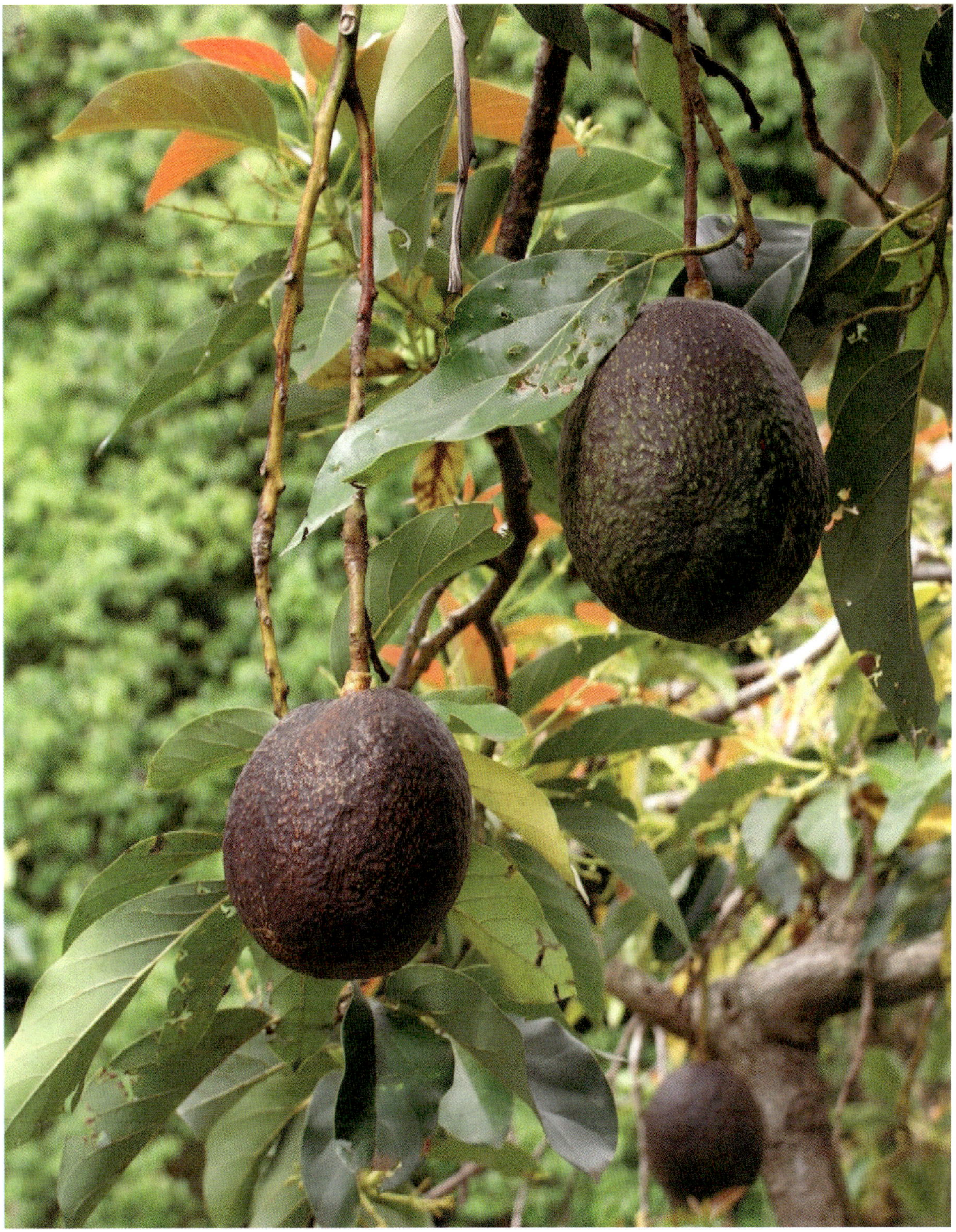

Bachelor's Buttons(Centaurea cyanus) a.k.a. devil's flower, red campion

Feminine. Venus. Water. Deity: Robin Goodfellow

Love.

Women wear this flower on their breast to attract love.

Balm, Lemon(Melissa officinalis) a.k.a. bee balm, lemon basalm, melissa, sweet balm, sweet melissa

Feminine. Moon. Water. Deity: Diana

Love. Success. Healing, especially for those with mental or nervous disorders.

Use in love charms and spells to attract a partner. Opens one to the divine love of the Goddess. Gives energy to make one more desirable to the opposite sex.

Balm of Gilead(Commiphora opobalsamum) a.k.a. balsam tree

Feminine. Venus. Water.

Love, Manifestations, Protection, Healing.

Carry the buds to mend a broken heart. Also steep them in red wine for a love potion. One of the best forms of magickal oils to be used to dress candles in magickal healing.

Bamboo(Bambusa Vulgaris)

Masculine. Deity: Hina

Protection, Luck, Hex-Breaking, Wishes.

Excellent for magick wands, representing all four elements. "Growing up from the earth through water, it passes through the sky as it reaches toward the fire of the Sun." Crush the wood to a powder and burn for protection — or grow by the house for good fortune.

Banana (Musa sapientum)

Feminine. Venus. Water.

Fertility. Cures impotency.

Use leaves, flowers, and fruits in prosperity and money spells.

Banyan(Ficus benghalensis) aka Indian fig tree, vada tree

Masculine. Jupiter. Air. Deity: Maui

Luck.

Barley(Hordeum spp.)

    Feminine. Venus. Earth. Deity: Venus

    Love, Healing, Protection.

    Use the grain or barley water in love spells.

Basil(Ocimum Basilicum) a.k.a. Witches herb, American dittany, St. Joseph's herb

Masculine. Mars. Fire. Deity: Vishnu, Ezrulie

Love, Exorcism, Wealth, Flying, Protection.

Causes sympathy between two people and soothes tempers between lovers. Add to love sachets and incenses. Place in cash register or on doorsill of business to attract customers. Use when invoking elemental salamanders or communing with dragons. Also used for courage.

Bay(Laurus nobilis) a.k.a. bay laurel, laurel, sweet bay

   Masculine. Sun. Fire.

Protection, Psychic Powers, Healing, Purification, Strength.

Used in clairvoyance and wisdom brews. Place leaves under pillow for prophetic dreams. Burn to cause vision. Attracts love and romance. Use to consecrate musical instruments. Bay leaves impart strength to athletes. Write wishes on bay leaves and burn.

Bean(Phaseolus spp.)

Masculine. Mercury. Air. Deities: Demeter, Cardea.

Protection, Exorcism, Wart Charming, Reconciliations, Potency, Love.

Used in rattles, they scare away bad spirits. Rub a dried bean on warts during the waning Moon. As you do so, say "As this bean decays, So wort, fall away!"

Bedstraw(Galium triflorum)

Feminine. Venus. Water.

Worn or carried to attract love.

Beech(Fagus sylvatica)

Feminine. Saturn.

Wishes

Beet(Beta vulgaris)

Feminine. Saturn. Earth.

Love.

Use as an ink in love magick, also as a blood substitute.

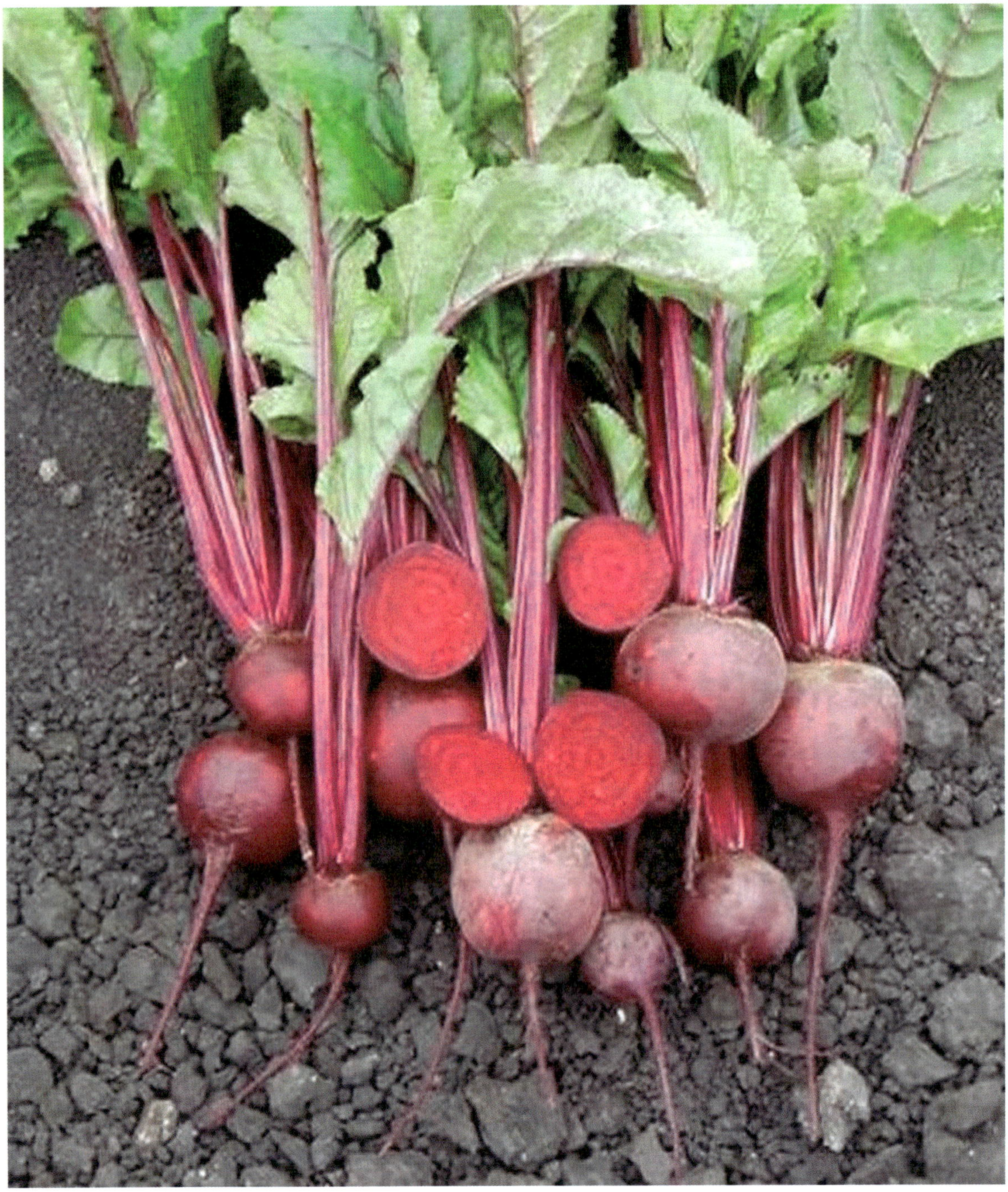

Belladonna(Atropa belladonna) a.k.a. banewort, witches berry, sorcerer's berry, deadly nightshade, death's herb, devil's cherries *Poison*

Feminine. Saturn. Water. Deities: Hecate, Bellona, Circe

Highly toxic. All parts of the plant are extremely poisonous. Encourages astral projection and produces visions, but belladonna is best avoided. A primary ingredient in flying ointments. Used in funeral rituals to aspurge the circle, helping the deceased to let go and move forward. Used to invoke Circe. Gather berries when they are ripe (around Samhain.) Store with onyx. Medicinally, it has been used as a sedative.

As every part of the plant is extremely poisonous, neither leaves, berries, nor root should be handled if there are any cuts or abrasions on the hands. The root is the most poisonous, the leaves and flowers less so, and the berries, except to children, least of all. It is said that an adult may eat two or three berries without injury, but dangerous symptoms appear if more are taken, and it is wiser not to attempt the experiment. Though so powerful in its action on the human body, the plant seems to affect some of the lower animals but little. Rabbits, sheep, goats and swine eat the leaves with impunity, and birds often eat the seeds without any apparent effect, but cats and dogs are very susceptible to the poison. — Grieve's Modern Herbal

Benzoin(Styrax benzoin)

Masculine. Sun. Air. Deities: Venus, Aphrodite, Mut.

Purification, Prosperity. Provides focus. Enhances concentration.

Useful in astral travel (protects spirit while travelling). Promotes generosity. Brings increased success to any magickal working or to attain magickal goals. Used as a base for incense. Make an incense of benzoin, cinnamon, and basil to attract customers to your place of business.

Bergamot, Orange(Mentha citrata) a.k.a. orange mint, bergamot

Masculine. Mercury. Air.

Money.

Put leaves in wallet or purse to attract money. Rub fresh leaves on money before spending.

Be-Still(Thevetia nereifolia) a.k.a. trumpet flower, yellow oleander

POISON

Wear beans as a talisan to attract luck.

Betony, Wood(Betonica officinalis) a.k.a. bishopwort, lousewort, purple betony

Masculine. Jupiter. Fire.

Protection, Purification, Love.

Placed under the pillow, it shields the sleeper from dreams. Throw in the Midsummer fire and jump through the smoke to purify the body. Very powerful in its ability to protect against dark and negative energy.

Birch(Betula alba)

    Feminine. Venus. Water. Deity: Thor

    Protection, Exorcism, Purification.

The traditional broom of the witch is made from birch twigs. Since birch is sacred to Thor, it is best to take the bark after the tree has been "kissed" by Thor, that is, hit by lightning. A circular grove of oak trees is among the most magickal of sites.

Bistort(Polygonum bistorta) a.k.a. dragonwort, snakeweed, sweet dock

Feminine. Saturn. Earth

Psychic Powers, Fertility.

Carry bistort if you wish to conceive. Burn with frankincense to increase psychic powers or when using divination. Add to money and wealth incenses.

Bittersweet (Celastrus scandens)

Masculine. Mercury. Air

Protection, Healing

Blackberry(Rubus villosus)

Feminine. Venus. Water. Deity: Bridget

Healing, Money, Protection.

Bake blackberry pies at Lammas. Use leaves and berries in spells of wealth. Dry fruit and powder it for use in magickal healing potions. Weave pentagrams from the brambles to hang in the home for protection.

Bladderwrack(Fucus visiculos) a.k.a. kelp, sea spirit, seawrack

Feminine. Moon. Water.

Protection, Sea Spells, Wind Spells, Money, Psychic Powers.

Fill a small jar with whiskey, add kelp and cap tightly. Place in kitchen window to ensure a steady flow of money in the household.

Bleeding Heart(Dicentra spectabilis or D. formosa)

Feminine. Venus. Water

Love.

When grown, the plant brings love. If growing indoors, plant a penny in the soil to offset negative vibrations. (For some reason, this plant emits negativity when grown indoors — maybe because love needs freedom to grow?) Lore: crush the flower. If the juice is red, your love has a heart full of love for you. If it is white, he or she does not.

Bloodroot(Sanguinaria canadensis) a.k.a. king root, red root

POISON

Masculine. Mars. Fire.

Love, Protection, Purification.

Wear or carry the root to draw love and to avert evil spells and negativity.

Bluebell(Campanula rotundifolia) a.k.a. harebell

    Luck, Truth.

    Anyone who wears a bluebell is compelled to tell the truth in all matters. Plant on graves. Comforts those left behind.

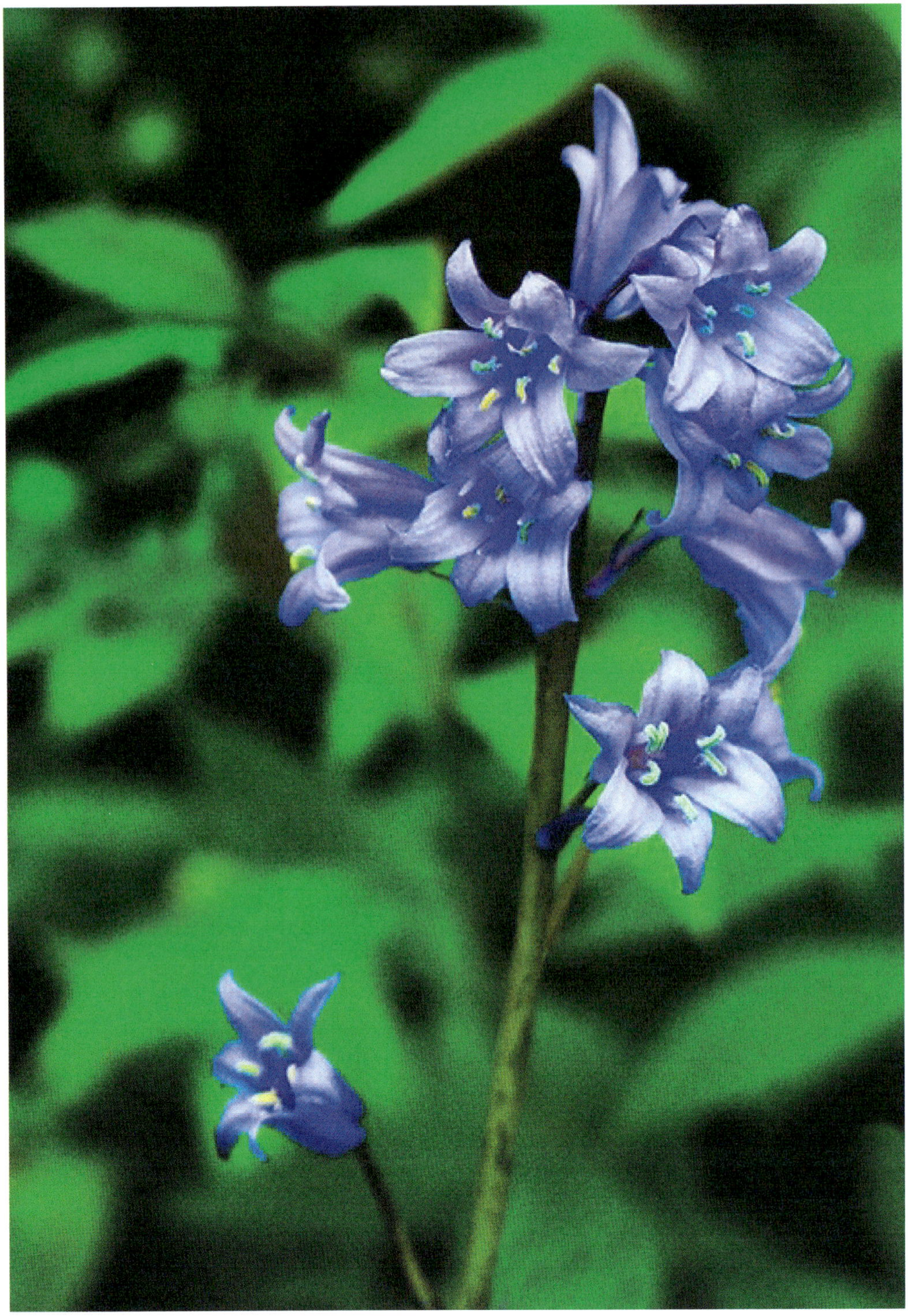

Blueberry(Vaccinum frondosum) a.k.a. bilberry

Protection.

Keeping blueberries under the doormat will keep away undesirables. Eat blueberry pie when under attack. This gets the protection inside you and increases the herb's protectiveness.

Blue Flag(Iris versicolor) a.k.a. iris, liver lily, poison lily, flag lily, fleur-de-lys *POISON*

Feminine. Venus. Water.

Money.

Carry the root for financial gain. Place in cash registers to increase business.

Bodhi(Ficus religiosa) a.k.a. bo-tree, peepul tree, pipul

Gender. Jupiter. Air. Deities: Vishnu, Buddha

Fertility, Protection, Wisdom, Meditation.

Boneset(Eupatorium perfoliatum) a.k.a. Indian sage, feverwort, sweating plant, teasel, wood boneset

Feminine. Saturn. Water.

Protection. Exorcism.

Borage (Borago officinalis)

Masculine. Jupiter. Air.

Courage.

Drink a tea for psychic powers. No matter how difficult the times, borage will always lift spirits.

Bracken(Pteridium aquilinum)

    Masculine. Mercury. Air.

    Healing, Rain Magick, Prophetic Dreams.

    If bracken is burned outside, rain will fall. Place the root under the pillow and solutions to problems will appear in dreams. Also used for fertility and protection.

Brazil Nut(Bertholletia excellsa)

Masculine. Mercury. Air.

Carry as a talisman for love.

Briony(Bryony, spp.) a.k.a. wild hops, wild vine, wood vine, gout root, mad root, snake grape

Masculine. Mars. Fire.

Image Magick, Money, Protection.

Often used as a substitute for the rare mandrake root in poppet magick. Money placed near briony root will increase, as long as it is left there. Hang in houses to protect against bad weather.

Bromeliad(Crypanthus, spp.) a.k.a. chameleon star, Earth star

Masculine. Sun. Air.

Protection, Money.

Grow in the home for protection, money, and luxuries.

Broom(Cytisus scoparius) a.k.a. besom, basam, broom tops, Irish broom, Scotch broom

POISON

Masculine. Mars. Air.

Purification, Protection, Wind Spells, Divination.

Makes an excellent ritual or handfasting broom. Use to create sacred space. Blooms bring good fortune and plenty. To raise the winds, throw broom into the air while invoking the spirits of the Air. To calm the winds, burn broom and bury the ashes. An infusion sprinkled throughout the house exorcises poltergists.

Buchu(Agathosma betulia or Barosma betulina) a.k.a. buku, oval buchu, short buchu

Feminine. Moon. Water.

Psychic Powers, Prophetic Dreams.

Drink to foretell the future. Mix with frankincense and burn before sleep for prophetic dreams (only a small amount in the bedroom).

Buckthorn (Rhammus spp.)

Feminine. Saturn. Water.

Protection, Exorcism, Wishes, Legal Matters.

Buckwheat(Fagopyrum spp.) a.k.a. beechwheat, French wheat, Saracen corn

Feminine. Venus. Earth.

Money, Protection.

Form magick circles with the flour for protection. Add a few grains to money incenses and keep in the kitchen to guard against poverty.

Burdock(Arctium lappa) a.k.a. beggar's buttons, cockleburr, great burdock

Feminine. Venus. Water.

Protection, Healing

Cactus(all species)

Protection, Chastity.

Cactus spines are used in witches bottles for protection. Carry or bury to release their protective powers.

Calamus(Acorus calamus) a.k.a. myrtle flag, sweet cane, sedge, sweet flag, sweet grass, sweet sedge

Feminine. Moon. Water.

POISON

Luck, Healing, Money, Protection.

String beads and wear for healing. Use powdered root in incenses and sachets. Used to strengthen and bind spells. Growing the plant brings good luck.

Camellia(Camellia japonica)

   Feminine. Moon. Water.

   Brings riches and luxury. Place fresh blossoms in water on altar during money and prosperity riches.

Camphor (Cinnamomum camphora)

Feminine. Moon. Water.

Chastity, Health, Divination.

A bag of camphor hung around the neck keeps flus and colds away. Use in divinatory incenses.

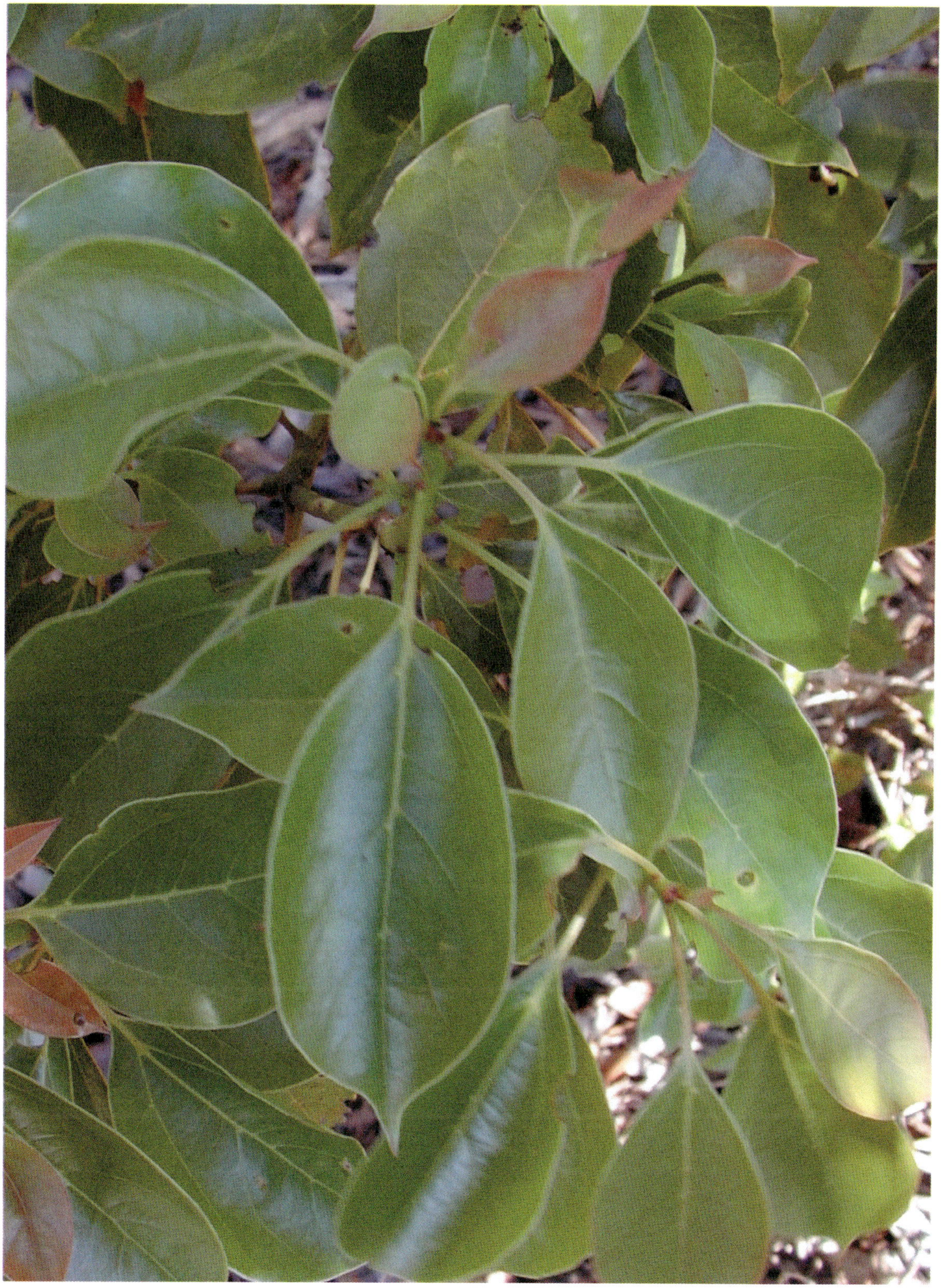

Caraway (Carum carvi)

Masculine. Mercury. Air.

Protection, Lust, Health, Anti-Theft, Mental Powers.

Any object which holds some caraway seeds is theft-free. Induces lust when baked into breads, cookies, or cakes. The seeds strengthen the memory.

Cardamom (Elettario caramomum)

Feminine. Venus. Water.

Lust, Love.

Add ground seeds to warmed wine for a quick lust potion. Bake in apple pies and add to sachets and incenses to induce love.

Carnation(Dianthus carophyllus) a.k.a. jove's flower, gillies, gilliflower, sops-in-wine

Masculine. Sun. Fire.

Protection, Strength, Healing.

Use in all-purpose protection spells. Gives strength and energy to the sick. Place fresh carnation on the altar during healing spells and add dried flowers to healing sachets and incenses.

Carob(Jacaranda procera or Prosopis dulcis) a.k.a. caroba, carobina, carobinha

Protection, Health.

Wear or carry.

Carrot(Dancus carota)

Masculine. Mars. Fire.

Fertility, Lust.

Women should eat the seeds to become pregnant. Eat carrots to promote lust and cure impotence.

Cascara Sagrada(Rhamnus purshiana) a.k.a. sacred bark

Legal Matters, Money, Protection.

Sprinkle infusion around your home before going to court. It will help you win your case.

Cashew(Anacardium occidentale)

Masculine. Sun. Fire.

Money.

Castor(Ricinus communis) a.k.a. palma christi, palms christi root

POISON

Protection.

Catnip(Nepeta cataria) a.k.a. catmint, cat's wort, field balm, nepeta, nip, catnep

Feminine. Venus. Water. Deity: Bast.

Cat Magick, Love, Beauty, Happiness.

Give to your cat to create a psychic bond between the two of you. Use in love sachets with rose petals. Attracts good spirits and great luck. Used in beauty and happiness spells. Large pressed leaves are used for bookmarks in magickal texts. Mix with dragon's blood in an incense to rid oneself of bad habits or behavioral problems.

Cattail(Typah spp.)

Masculine. Mars. Fire.

Lust.

Carry if you don't like sex, but want to.

Cedar(Cedrus libani or C. spp.)

Masculine. Sun. Fire.

Healing, Purification, Money, Protection.

The smoke is purifying and chases away bad dreams. Keep a piece in the wallet to draw money and in all money incenses. Add to love sachets and Burn for psychic powers.

Celandine(Chelidonium majus) a.k.a. devil's milk, kenning wort, swallow-wort, tetterwort

Masculine. Sun. Fire.

Protection, Escape, Happiness, Legal Matters.

Aids in escaping unwarranted imprisonment or entrapment. Wear next to the skin and replace every three days. Cures depression, brings happiness when worn. Wear to court to win the favor of the jury.

Celery(Apium graveolens)

    Masculine. Mercury. Fire.

    Mental Powers, Lust, Psychic Powers.

    Chew seeds to aid concentration or in dream pillows to induce sleep. Burned with orris root, seeds increase psychic powers. Eat stalk to induce lust.

Centaury(Centaurium spp.) a.k.a. christ's ladder, feverwort

Masculine. Sun. Fire.

Burn to drive off snakes.

Chamomile(Anthemis nobilis) a.k.a. ground apple, roman camomile, maythn, whig plant

Masculine. Sun. Water

Money, Sleep, Love, Purification.

Sprinkle around property to remove curses and spells cast against you.

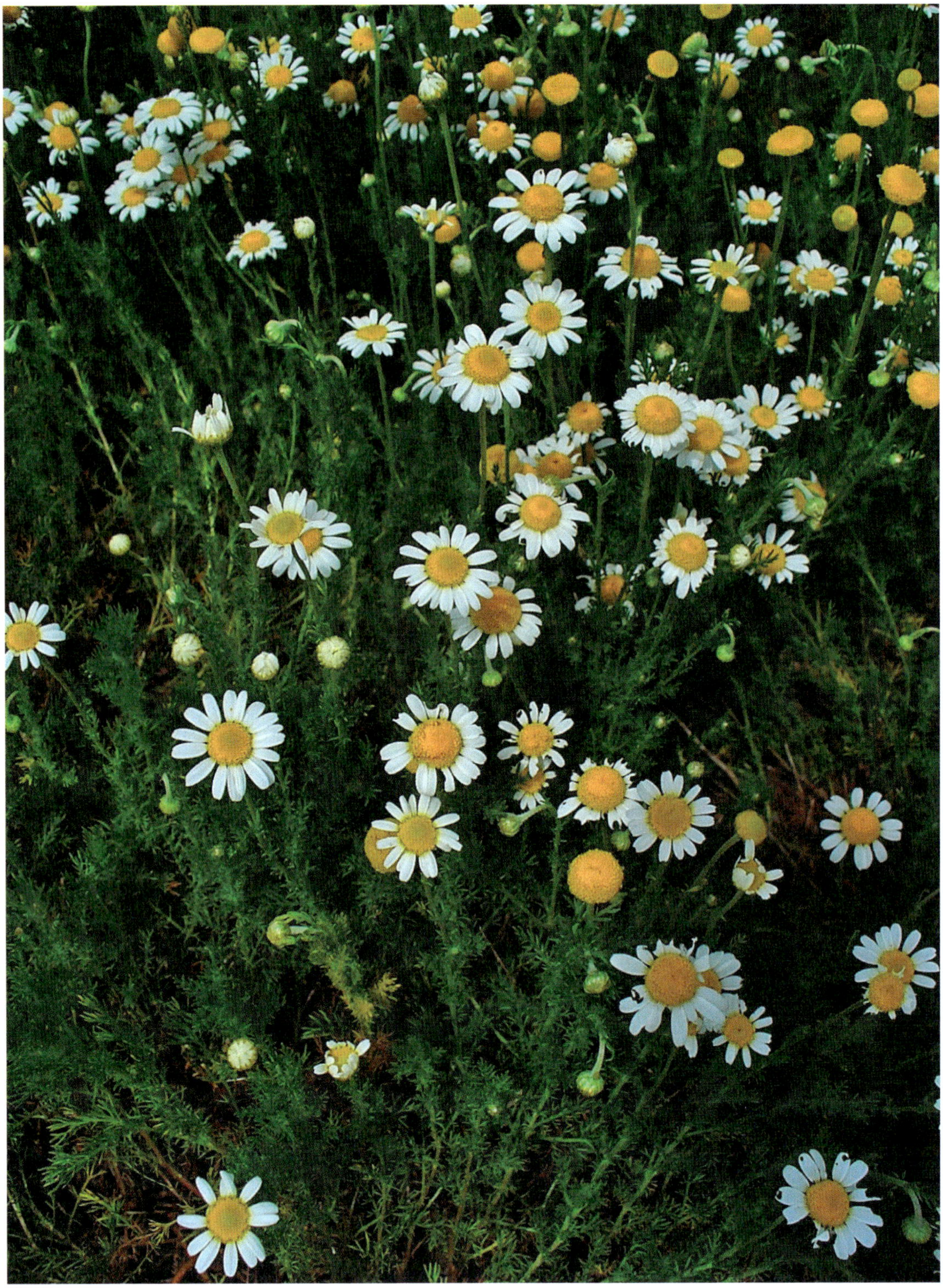

Cherry(Prunus avium) a.k.a. sweet cherry

Feminine. Venus. Water.

Love, Divination.

Chestnut(Castanea spp.)

Masculine. Jupiter. Fire.

Love.

Chickweed(Stellaria media) a.k.a. adder's mouth, starweed, starwort, stitchwort, tongue grass

Feminine. Moon. Water.

Fertility, Love

Chicory(Cichorium intybus) a.k.a. succory, wild cherry, wild succory

Masculine. Sun. Air.

Removing Obstacles, Invisibility, Favors, Frugality.

Carry to remove all obstacles that might crop up in your life. Rub juice on body to obtain favors from great persons.

Chili Pepper(Capsicum spp.) a.k.a. red pepper

Masculine. Mars. Fire.

Fidelity, Hex Breaking, Love.

China Berry(Melia azederach)

POISON

Carry seeds for luck and to bring change into your life.

Chrysanthemum(Anacylus pyrethrum) a.k.a. mum

Masculine. Sun. Fire.

Protection.

Promotes mental health. Use in rituals of death and dying.

Cinnamon(Cinnamonum zeylanicum) a.k.a. sweet wood

Masculine. Sun. Fire. Deities: Venus, Aphrodite

Spirituality, Success, Healing, Power, Psychic Powers, Lust, Protection, Love.

Empower with tourmaline. Enhancing skills of prophecy through channeling, working through an oracle, or through divination. When burned as an incense, it raises high spiritual vibrations. Aids in healing. Draws money. Stimulates psychic power and produces protective vibrations. Great in sachets and amulets.

Cinquefoil(Potentilla canadensis or P. reptans) a.k.a. crampweed, five finger blossom, five finger grass, goosegrass, silverweed, potentilla

Masculine. Jupiter. Fire.

The five points of the leaves represent love, money, health, power, and wisdom.

If carried, all these will be granted. Good for love magick and to promote an abundant harvest. Contains the energy to manifest one's ideas. An ingredient in mediaeval flying ointments.

Citron (Citrus medica)

Masculine. Sun. Air.

Psychic Powers, Healing.

Clove(Syzygium aromaticum or Caryophyllus aromatica)

Masculine. Jupiter. Fire.

Protection, Exorcism, Love, Money.

Burn as an incense. Worn or carried, they attract the opposite sex.

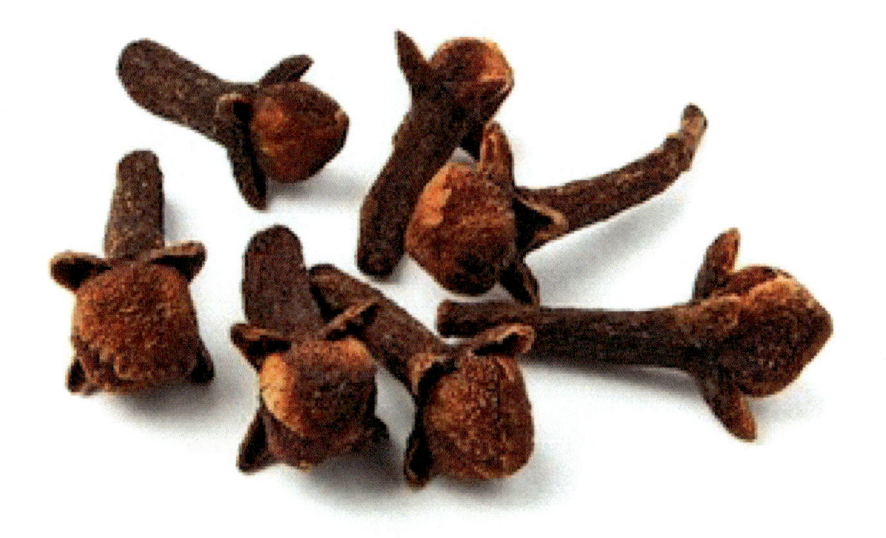

Clover(Trifolium spp.) a.k.a. shamrock, trefoil, three-leaved grass

Masculine. Mercury. Air.

Protection, Love, Money, Fidelity, Exorcism, Success.

Coconut(Cocus necifera)

Feminine. Moon. Water.

Purification, Protection, Chastity

Coffee(Coffea Arabica)

Mercury. Uranus.

Ritual stimulant.

Aztec, Mayan, and Incan peoples all revered the berry of this plant.

Cohosh, Black(Cimicifuga racemosa) a.k.a. black snake root, bugbane, squawroot

Masculine.

Love, Courage, Protection, Potency

Coltsfoot(Tussilago Farfara) a.k.a. ass's foot, British tobacco, bull's foot, butterbur, Coughwort

Feminine. Venus. Water.

Use in love sachets and spells of peace and tranquility.

Love, Visions.

Chrysanthemum

    Feminine. Venus. Water.

    Love, Courage.

    Rub on hands for courage and daring or carry it. Seeds can be used in love perfume. Pulverize seeds and rub on hands to attract love. Practitioners of animal magick, those working with eagles (aquila=eagle), or those wishing to invoke the protection of deity through the realm of birds may work with this herb.

Comfrey(Symphytum officinale) a.k.a. boneset, bruisewort, knit back, knit bone, slippery root

Feminine. Saturn. Water.

Good for any magickal healing. Worn or carried, it ensures safety during travel. The root is used in money spells.

Copal(Bursera odorata)

    Masculine. Sun. Fire.

    Love, Purification.

    Added to love and purification incenses. A piece of copal can represent the heart in poppets.

Coriander(Coriandrum sativum) a.k.a. Chinese parsley, cilantro

Masculine. Mars. Fire.

Love, Health, Healing.

Used in love sachets and spells. Add the powdered seeds to warm wine to make a lust potion. Protects gardeners and all in their households. Gather at harvest and hang in the home for protection. The seeds promote peace between people who are unable to get along. Use it in drinks or crushed in incense. Helps one find romance and is an excellent herb to add to an elixir when the Great Rite is celebrated. Throw instead of rice at handfastings or add to the handfasting cake.

Corn(Zea Mays) a.k.a. maize, seed of seeds, sacred mother

Feminine. Venus. Earth.

Protection, Luck, Divination.

Represents fertility and is used to invoke Mother Earth. Used at Mabon and Lammas in ritual, it teaches the mystery of life, death, and rebirth.

Cornflower(Centaurea Cyanus) a.k.a. blue bottle, bluecap, bluet

Venus. Saturn. Deity: Flora, Chiron.

Patron herb of herbalists. Blue leaves make a lovely ink for Book of Shadows.

Cotton (Gossypium barbadense)

Feminine. Moon. Earth.

Luck, Healing, Protection, Rain, Fishing Magick.

Place cotton on an aching tooth to take away pain. Planted or scattered in yard, it keeps ghosts away. Burning cotton causes rain.

Cowslip(Primula veris) a.k.a. arthritica, fairy cup, lady's key, buckles

Feminine. Venus. Water. Deity: Freya.

Healing, Youth, Treasure Finding.

Place it beneath the front porch to discourage visitors. Preserves youth, and restores it when lost. The odor is healing, and holding a bunch will locate hidden treasure. Sacred to Freya, and can be used to invoke her. Some believe the path to Freya will lead one to earthbound treasures and abundance.

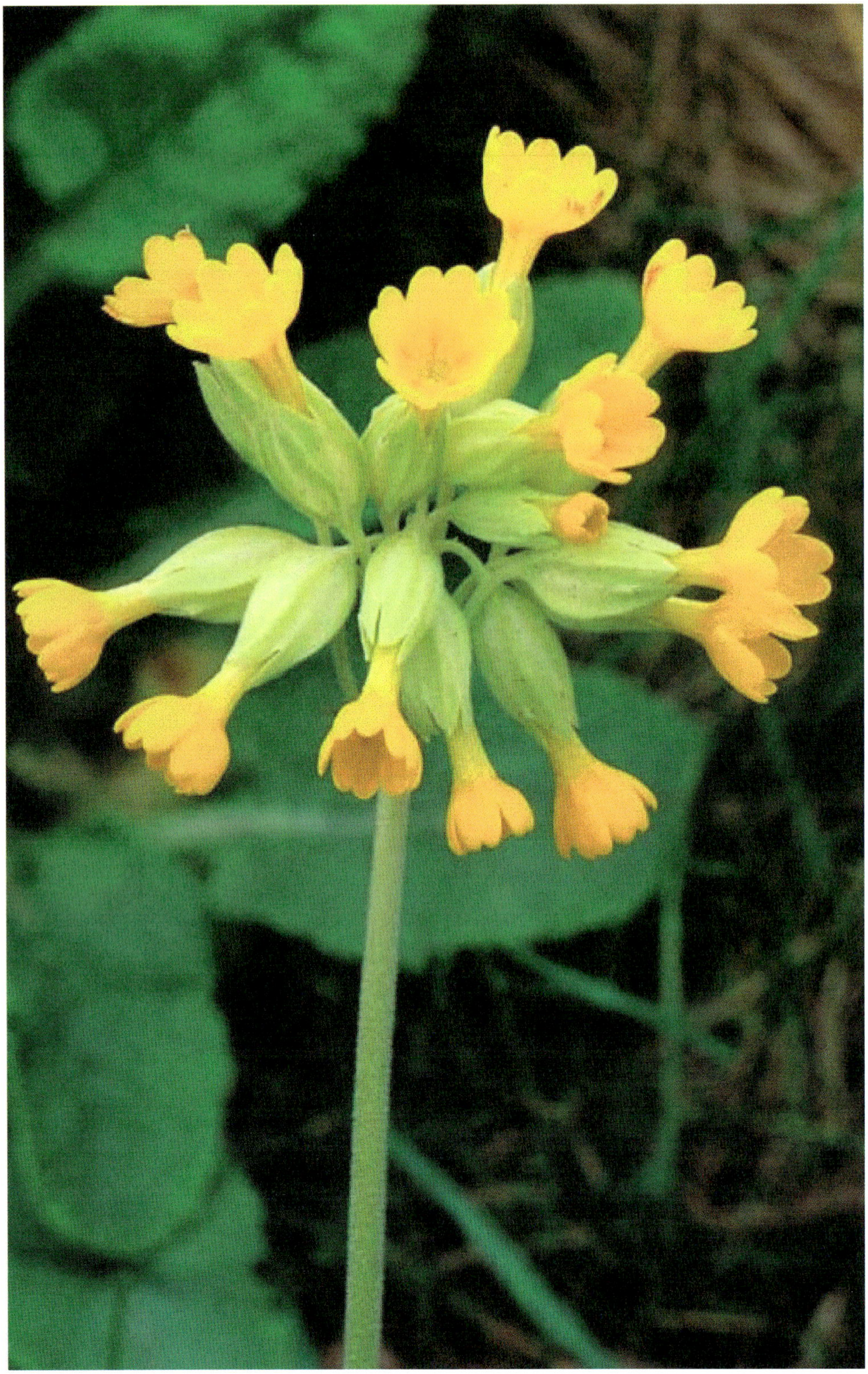

Crocus(Crocus vernus)

Feminine. Venus. Water.

Burn in a censor with alum to see a vision of the thief who robbed you. Love, Visions.

Cucumber(Cucumis sativus) a.k.a. cowcucumber

Feminine. Moon. Water. Deity: Uttu (Sumerian)

Chastity, Healing, Fertility.

Cooling and soothing to the psyche. Slices laid on eyes assists astral travel. Fruit hinders lust. Peel on head relieves pain of headache.

Cumin(Cumimum Cyminum) a.k.a. cumino, cumino aigro

Masculine. Mars. Fire.

Protection, Fidelity, Exorcism, Anti-theft.

Burned with frankincense for protection and scattered on the floor (sometimes with salt) to drive out evil. Used in love spells. When given to a lover, promotes fidelity. Cumin seed steeped in wine makes a lust potion.

Curry(Murraya Koenigii)

Masculine. Mars. Fire.

Protection.

Burn the specific plant, not the mixture of spices, to repel evil at night.

Cyclamen(Cyclamen spp.) a.k.a. groundbread, sow bread, swine bread

Feminine. Venus. Water. Deities: Hecate

Fertility, Protection, Happiness, Lust.

Add to handfasting or wedding cake.

Cypress(Cupressus sempervirens) a.k.a. Tree of Death

Feminine. Saturn. Earth. Deities: Hecate, Hebe, Mithras, Pluto, Aphrodite, Ashtoreth, Artemis, Apollo, Cupid, Jupiter, Zoroaster.

Longevity, Healing, Comfort, Protection.

Wear at time of crisis. Taken to funerals, eases grief and calms mind. Throw a sprig of cypress into a grave to give the deceased luck and love in the hereafter.

Daffodil

Love, Fertility, Luck

Daisy

Lust, Luck

Damiana

Lust, Love, Visions

Dandelion

Divination, Wishes, Calling Spirits

Deerstongue

Lust, Psychic Powers

Dill

Protection, Money, Lust, Luck

Dock

Healing, Fertility, Money

Dogbane(Apocynum adrosaemifolium)

Use the flowers in magickal love mixtures.

Dogwood(Pyiscidia erythrina)

Moon, Pluto. Pisces. Deity: Consus

Wishes, Protection.

Keeps writings and meetings secret, therefore is an excellent herb for the Book of Shadows. An oil of the flowers is priceless in sealing letters and keeping unintended eyes from secret writings. Powdered flowers and dried bark may be used as incense. Place the sap of the dogwood onto a handkerchief on Midsummer Eve. This will grant any wish you have as long as you carry it faithfully. Dogwood leaves or wood can be placed in protective amulets.

Dragon's Blood (Daemomorops Draco)

Masculine. Mars. Fire.

Love, Protection, Exorcism, Potency.

Used in homemade magickal inks. Burn the resin to entice errant lovers to return. A stick placed under the pillow will cure impotency. A powerful protectant when sprinkled around the house or burned as incense. A pinch added to to other incenses will increase their potency.

Dulse

Lust, Harmony

Dutchman's Britches

Love

Ebony

Protection, Power

Echinacea

    Strengthening Spells

Edelwiess

    Invisibility, Bullet-Proofing

Elder

    Exorcism, Protection, Healing, Prosperity, Peace

Elecampane

    Love, Protection, Psychic Powers

Elm

    Love

Endive

    Love, Lust

Eucalyptus

    Healing, Protection

Eyebright
Mental Powers, Psychic Powers

Fennel
Protection, Healing, Purification

Fenugreek
Money

Fern
Rain Making, Protection, Luck, Riches, Health, Exorcism

Feverfew
Protection

Fig
Divination, Fertility, Love

Figwort
Health, Protection

Flax

Money, Protection, Beauty, Psychic Powers, Healing

Fleabane

Exorcism, Protection, Chastity

Foxglove (Digitalis purpurea) a.k.a. deadmen's bells, dog's finger, fairy thimbles, fox bells, witches bells, witches thimbles

POISON

Feminine. Venus. Water.

Protection.

Brings true magick to your garden by attracting faeries and plant devas. Assists in communion with the Underworld. Collect the juice of the herb under a favorable moon sign. Mark the very center of your circle with the juice and wait there to see the realm of faery.

Frankincense

Protection, Exorcism, Spirituality

Gardenia

Love, Peace, Healing, Spirituality

Garlic

Protection, Healing, Exorcism, Lust, Anti-Theft

Gentian

   Love, Power

Geranium

   Fertility, Love, Health, Protection

Ginger

   Love, Money, Success, Power

Ginseng

   Love, Wishes, Healing, Beauty, Protection, Lust

Goats Rue

   Healing, Health

Goldenrod

   Money, Divination

Goldenseal

   Healing, Money

Gorse

    Protection, Money

Gotu Kola

    Meditation

Gourd

    Protection

Grain

    Protection

Grape

    Fertility, Garden Magick, Mental Powers, Money

Grass

    Psychic Powers, Protection

Ground Ivy

    Divination

Groundsel

Health, Healing

Hawthorn

Fertility, Chastity, Fishing Magick, Happiness

Hazel

Luck, Fertility, Anti-Lightning, Protection, Wishes

Heather(Calluna Vulgaris) a.k.a. heath

Feminine. Venus. Water. Deity: Isis, Osiris, Venus

Protection, Rain Making, Luck.

Robert Graves said heather is "a suitable tree for the inititation of Scottish witches." Brings one in touch with divinity and increases physical beauty. Wearing an amulet of the wood will bring a long physical life and put one in touch with the truly immortal soul. A valuable herb for those who pursue initiatory paths. Unfolds the inner self. Carried, it will guard against rape or other violent crimes or just to bring good luck. (White heather is best here.) When burned with fern will attract rain.

Heliotrope

Exorcism, Prophetic Dreams, Healing, Wealth, Invisibility

Hellebore, Black(Helleborus niger) a.k.a. Melampode

Feminine. Saturn. Water.

Poison

Protection.

Provides an aura or mantle of invisibility. The safest use of this herb is to place pieces of the root or dried berries in an amulet or magick pouch. Used to bless farm animals and pets. Good for working with familiars — but please don't breathe the fumes or ingest!

Hemlock(Conium maculatum) a.k.a. herb bennet, poison parsley, spotted hemlock, water parsley

Feminine. Saturn. Water. Deity: Hecate

Poison

Destroys sexual drive. Induces astral projection. Juice rubbed on magickal blades empower and purify them. Used in medievel flying ointments.

Hemp

Healing, Love, Vision, Meditation

Henbane(Hyosycamus niger) a.k.a. black nightshade, devil's eye, henbells, poison tobacco, hogsbean

Feminine. Saturn. Water. *Poison*

A love-bringing herb when worn. Traditionally used in ointments and brews. Induces delirium. Used with wisdom, it could be an excellent herb for consecrating ceremonial vessels. Attracts hares, therefore would be an excellent herb for those who raise rabbits.

Henna (Lawsonia inermis)

Jupiter.

Healing.

Place on forehead to relieve headache. Attracts love if worn near the heart. Protects from illness and from evil eye. A body adornment originating in the Mediterranean. Modern witches use as a ritual adornment, especially for the Great Rite and other important ritual occasions. Henna mixed with olive oil, massaged on the penis at the rising and setting suns promotes virility.

Hibiscus

Lust, Love, Divination

Hickory

Legal Matters

High John the Conqueror

Money, Love, Success, Happiness

Holly (Ilex aquifolium or I. opaca)

Masculine. Mars. Fire. Deity: Holly King

Protection, Anti-Lightning, Luck, Dream Magick.

One of the best protective herbs. The wood of the holly is very well suited for the handle of the ritual knife as it both attracts and repels energies. It is powerful when defense is needed in circle while preserving the gentleness within it. Holly water is sprinkled on newborn babies to protect them. Carried by men, it promotes luck. (Ivy is the corresponding plant of luck for women). Decorate the house with it at Yule for good luck.

After midnight on a Friday, without making a sound, gather nine holly leaves, preferably from a non-spiny plant (one that has smooth leaves). Wrap these up in a white cloth using nine knots to tie the ends together. Place this beneath your pillow, and your dreams will come true. — Cunningham's Encyclopedia of Magickal Herbs

Honesty

Money, Repelling Monsters

Honeysuckle(Lonicera caprifolium) a.k.a. goat's leaf, woodbine

Masculine. Jupiter. Earth

Money, Psychic Powers, Protection.

Ring green candles with honeysuckle flowers to attract money or place them in a vase in the house for the same purpose. Lightly crush flowers and rub on forehead to heighten psychic powers. The extracted oil is best for increasing spiritual sight. It enhances understanding of images and impressions collected in the astral. Connects one with the mysteries of the Cauldron of Cerridwen. In ritual, dried, powdered bark may be used as incense.

Hops

Healing, Sleep

Horehound

Protection, Mental Powers, Exorcism, Healing

Horse Chestnut

Money, Healing

Horseradish

Purification, Exorcism

Horsetail

Snake Charming, Fertility

Houseleek

Luck, Protection, Love

Huckleberry

Luck, Protection, Dream Magick, Hex Breaking

Hyacinth

Love, Protection, Happiness

Hydrangea

    Hex Breaking

Hyssop

    Purification, Protection

Indian Paint Brush

    Love

Iris

    Purification, Wisdom

Irish Moss

    Money, Luck, Protection

Ivy

    Protection, Healing

Jasmine

    Love, Money, Prophetic Dreams

Jobs Tears

Healing, Wishes, Luck

Joe Pye Weed

Love, Respect

Juniper

Protection, Anti-Theft, Love, Exorcism, Health

Kava-Kava

Visions, Protection, Luck

Knotweed

Binding, Health

Lady's Mantle

Love

Lady's Slipper

Protection

Larch

Protection, Anti-Theft

Larkspur

Health, Protection

Lavender

Love, Protection, Sleep, Chastity (with rosemary), Longevity, Purification, Happiness, Peace

Leek

Love, Protection, Exorcism

Lemon

Longevity, Purification, Love, Friendship

Lemongrass

Repel Snakes, Lust, Psychic Powers

Lemon Verbena

Purification, Love

Lettuce

Chastity, Protection, Love, Divination, Sleep

Licorice

Love, Lust, Fidelity

Life Everlasting

Longevity, Health, Healing

Lilac

Exorcism, Protection

Lily

Protection, Breaking Love Spells

Lily of the Valley

Mental Powers, Happiness

Lime

Healing, Love, Protection

Linden

Protection, Immortality, Luck, Love, Sleep

Liverwort

    Protection, Love

Loosestrife

    Peace, Protection

Lotus

    Protection, Lock-Opening

Lovage

    Love

Love Seed

    Friendship, Love

Lucky Hand

    Employment, Luck, Protection, Money, Travel

Mace

    Psychic Powers, Mental Powers

Magnolia

    Fidelity

Maidenhair

    Beauty, Love

Male Fern

    Luck, Love

Mallow

    Love, Protection, Exorcism

Mandrake(Mandragora officinale or Atropa Mandragora) aka herb of Circe, witches mannikin, wild lemon, sorceror's root *Poison*

    Masculine. Mercury. Fire. Deities: Circe, Diana, Hecate, Hathor, Saturn

    Protection, Love, Money, Fertility, Health.

    Few herbs are as steeped in magickal lore as mandrake. It is associated with the most intense practices of magick and especially well suited for love magick. It has great power as a visionary herb. It empowers visions, providing the impetus to bring them into manifestation. It intensifies the magick of any situation. A whole mandrake root placed in the home will bring protection and prosperity. Carried, it will attract love. The human shape of the root makes it well suited for use as poppet. (Substitute ash roots, apples, root of the briony,

or the American may apple if the cost is prohibitive). To activate a dried mandrake, place it on the altar undisturbed for three days. Then place it in warm water overnight. The root will then be activated and ready for any magickal purpose.

Maple

Love, Longevity, Money

Marigold (Calendula officinalis) aka calendula, drunkard, marybud, marygold

Masculine. Sun. Fire.

Protection, Prophetic Dreams, Legal Matters, Psychic Powers.

Aids visionary sight and helps find stolen property by producing a vision of the thief in the mind and the location of the stolen property. Dried petals may be used alone or mixed with dried incense to consecrate divination tools. Petals may be macerated in sunflower oil to make an oil of consecration. Adds a special, loving magick to rituals of death and dying. Carry marigold petals with a bay leaf to quiet gossip.

Marjoram

Protection, Love, Happiness, Health, Money

Mastic

Psychic Powers, Manifestations, Lust

May Apple(Podophyllum peltaltum) a.k.a. American mandrake, duck's foot, hog apple, racoon berry *Poison*

Masculine. Mercury. Fire.

Money.

Generally used as a substitution for European (true) mandrake. Its uses are practically identical, although the may apple is not related to the true mandrake.

Meadow Rue

Divination

Meadowsweet

Love, Divination, Peace, Happiness

Mesquite

Healing

Mimosa

Protection, Love, Prophetic Dreams, Purification

Mint

Money, Love, Lust, Healing, Exorcism, Travel, Protection

Mistletoe(Viscum Album) Witches broom, Thunderbesom, Holy wood, Golden bough

Masculine. Sun. Air. Deities: Balder, Apollo, Freya, Frigga, Venus, Odin

Protection, Love, Hunting, Fertility, Health, Exorcism.

Moonwort

Money, Love

Moss

Luck, Money

Mugwort(Artemisia vulgaris) a.k.a. Artemis herb, Artemisia, Felon herb, Muggons, Naughty Man, Sailor's Tobacco, St. John's Plant

Feminine. Venus. Earth. Deities: Artemis, Diana

Strength, Psychic Powers, Protection, Prophetic Dreams, Healing, Astral Projection.

Use a wash or the oil to consecrate or anoint crystal balls or any tool of divination. Produces visionary dreams and is a prime ingredient in dream pillows. Keeps one safe from dark forces. Protects children. Incense brings protection. Carried, it brings loved ones safely home from journeys. A tonic for the soul, it keeps us aware of our spiritual direction. Burn with sandalwood or wormwood during scrying sessions. A mugwort infusion sweetened with honey will enhance divination. Carried, it also increases lust and fertility.

Mulberry

   Protection, Strength

Mullein

   Courage, Protection, Health, Love, Divination, Exorcism

Mustard

   Fertility, Protection, Mental Powers

Myrrh

   Protection, Exorcism, Healing, Spirituality

Myrtle

   Love, Fertility, Youth, Peace, Money

Nettle

   Exorcism, Protection, Healing, Lust

Norfolk Island Pine

   Protection, Anti-Hunger

Nuts

Fertility, Prosperity, Love, Luck

Oak

Protection, Health, Money, Healing, Potency, Fertility, Luck

Oats

Money

Olive

Healing, Peace, Fertility, Potency, Protection, Lust

Onion

Protection, Exorcism, Healing, Money, Prophetic Dreams, Lust

Orange

Love, Divination, Luck, Money

Orchid

Love

Oregon Grape

Money, Prosperity

Orris (Iris florentina or Phizoma Iridis) a.k.a. Florentine Iris, Queen Elizabeth Root

Feminine. Venus. Water. Deities: Aphrodite, Isis, Osiris, Hera, Iris

Love, Protection, Divination.

The root is used to find and hold love. The root powder is known as "Love Drawing Powder." Protects from evil spirits. The roots and leaves hung in the house and added to the bath are good for personal protection. Make a pendulum with a small piece of the wood.

Palm, Date

Fertility, Potency

Pansy

Love, Rain Magick, Love, Divination

Papaya

Love, Protection

Parsley

Love, Protection, Purification

Passion Flower

Peace, Sleep, Friendship

Patchouli

Money, Fertility, Lust

Pea

Money, Love

Peach

Love, Exorcism, Longevity, Fertility, Wishes

Pear

Lust, Love

Pecan

Money, Employment

Pennyroyal

Strength, Protection, Peace

Peony

Protection, Exorcism

Pepper

Protection, Exorcism

Peppermint

Purification, Sleep, Love, Healing, Psychic Powers

Periwinkle(Vinca minor) a.k.a. Sorcerer's Violet, Blue Buttons *POISON*

Feminine, Venus, Water.

Patron herb of Wiccans. Love, Lust, Mental Powers, Money, Protection.

Best when gathered when the moon is one night old, nine nights old, 11 nights old, 13 nights old, or 30 nights old. The dried flowers may be added to any magickal mixture to enhance the working. Banishes negative energy. Makes one feel desirable. Add dried flowers or root to amulets to bring necessary changes to one's life to attract a loving partner. Plant on graves of children. Helps grieving parents heal from their loss. Keeps memory of lost child alive without unhealthy attachments.

Persimmon

Healing, Lust

Pimento

Love

Pine

Healing, Fertility, Protection, Exorcism, Money

Pineapple

Luck, Money, Chastity

Pistachio

Breaking Love Spells

Plum

Healing

Poke

Courage, Hex Breaking

Pomegranate

Divination, Luck, Wishes, Wealth, Fertility

Poplar

Money, Flying

Poppy

Fertility, Love, Sleep, Money, Luck, Invisibility

Potato

Image Magick, Healing

Prickly Ash

Love

Primrose

Protection, Love

Purslane

Sleep, Love, Luck, Protection, Happiness

Quince

Protection, Love, Happiness

Radish

Protection, Lust

Ragweed

    Courage

Raspberry

    Protection, Love

Rattlesnake Root

    Protection, Money

Rhubarb

    Protection, Fidelity

Rice

    Protection, Fidelity

Roots

    Protection, Power, Divination

Rose

    Love, Psychic Powers, Healing, Love, Divination, Luck, Protection

Rosemary

Protection, Love, Lust, Mental Powers, Exorcism, Purification, Healing, Sleep, Youth

Rowan

Psychic Powers, Healing, Protection, Success

Rue

Healing, Health, Mental Powers, Exorcism, Love

Rye

Love, Fertility

Saffron

Love, Healing, Happiness, Wind Raising, Lust, Strength, Psychic Powers

Sage

Immortality, Longevity, Wisdom, Protection, Wishes

Sagebrush

Purification, Exorcism

St. John's Wort
Health, Power, Protection, Strength, Love, Divination, Happiness

Sandalwood
Protection, Healing, Exorcism, Spirituality

Sarsaparilla
Love, Money

Sassafras
Health, Money

Savory, Summer
Mental Powers

Skullcap
Love, Fidelity, Peace

Senna
Love

Sesame

Money, Lust

Shallot

Purification

Skunk Cabbage

Legal Matters

Slippery Elm

Halts Gossip

Snakeroot

Luck, Money

Snakeroot, Black

Love, Lust, Money

Snapdragon

Protection

Solomon's Seal

Protection, Exorcism

Sorrel Wood

> **Healing, Health**

Southern Wood

> **Love, Lust, Protection**

Spanish Moss

> **Protection**

Spearmint

> **Healing, Love, Mental Powers**

Spiderwort

> **Love**

Spikenard

> **Love**

Star Anise

> **Psychic Powers, Luck**

Strawberry

    Love, Luck

Sugar Cane

    Love, Lust

Sunflower

    Fertility, Wishes, Health, Wisdom

Sweetgrass

    Calling Spirits

Sweetpea

    Friendship, Chastity, Courage, Strength

Tansy

    Health, Longevity

Tea

    Riches, Courage, Strength

Thistle

Strength, Protection, Hex Breaking, Healing

Thistle, Holy

Purification, Hex Breaking

Thistle, Milk

Snake enraging

Thyme

Health, Healing, Sleep, Psychic Powers, Love, Purification, Courage

Toadflax

Protection, Hex Breaking

Toadstool

Rain Making

Tobacco

Healing, Purification

Tonka Bean(Coumarouna odorata; Dipteryx odorata) a.k.a. Coumaria Nut, Tonqua, Tonquin Bean

DO NOT CONSUME. BELIEVED TO CAUSE CANCER

Feminine. Venus. Water.

Love. Money. Courage. Wishes.

Used extensively in love sachets and mixtures, and carried to attract love. Also worn or carried to attract money, bring luck, grant courage, and ward off illness.

Turmeric

Purification

Turnip

Protection, Ending Relationships

Uva Ursa

Psychic Workings

Valerian

Love, Sleep, Purification, Protection

Vanilla

Love, Lust, Mental Powers

Venus Flytrap

Protection, Love

Vervain (Verbena officinalis)

Feminine. Venus. Earth. Deities: Cerridwen, Mars, Venus, Aradia, Jupiter, Thor, Juno

The Witches Herb. Love, Protection, Purification, Peace, Money, Youth, Chastity, Sleep. Healing.

Empowers any magick, especially love spells. Enhances the dreaming process and is recommended for dream quests. Used to consecrate and empower any ritual tools. Protects from negative emotions and depression. Used in house and home blessings. Turns back negativity. In love spells: add to recipes to attract mates, find true love, achieve sexual fulfilment, work sexual magick, an for bringing extra bliss on the wedding night. The herb of poets, singers, and bards. Inspires artistry. Instills a love of learning. Best when gathered at Midsummer.

Vetch, Giant

Fidelity

Vetivert

Love, Hex Breaking, Luck, Money, Anti-Theft

Violet

Protection, Love, Lust, Luck, Wishes, Peace, Healing

Walnut

    Health, Mental Powers, Infertility, Wishes

Wheat

    Fertility, Money

Willow

    Love, Divination, Protection, Healing

Wintergreen

    Protection, Healing, Hex Breaking

Witch Hazel

    Protection, Chastity

Wolf's Bane

    see Aconite

Wood Rose

    Luck

Woodruff
Victory, Protection, Money

Wormwood
Psychic Powers, Protection, Love, Calling Spirits

Yarrow
Courage, Love, Psychic Powers, Exorcism

Yellow Evening Primrose
Hunting

Yerba Mate
Fidelity, Love, Lust

Yerba Santa
Beauty, Healing, Psychic Powers, Protection

Yucca
Transmutation, Protection, Purification

Printed in Great Britain
by Amazon